The House of Fog

Peter Brammer

A Samuel French Acting Edition

SAMUELFRENCH.COM
SAMUELFRENCH-LONDON.CO.UK

Copyright © 2014 by Peter Smith
All Rights Reserved

THE HOUSE OF FOG is fully protected under the copyright laws of the United States of America, the British Commonwealth, including Canada, and all other countries of the Copyright Union. All rights, including professional and amateur stage productions, recitation, lecturing, public reading, motion picture, radio broadcasting, television and the rights of translation into foreign languages are strictly reserved.

ISBN 978-0-573-11181-5

www.SamuelFrench.com
www.SamuelFrench-London.co.uk

For Production Enquiries

United States and Canada
Info@SamuelFrench.com
1-866-598-8449

United Kingdom and Europe
Plays@SamuelFrench-London.co.uk
020-7255-4302/01

Each title is subject to availability from Samuel French, depending upon country of performance. Please be aware that *THE HOUSE OF FOG* may not be licensed by Samuel French in your territory. Professional and amateur producers should contact the nearest Samuel French office or licensing partner to verify availability. For stock/ professional licensing enquiries please contact Samuel French.

CAUTION: Professional and amateur producers are hereby warned that *THE HOUSE OF FOG* is subject to a licensing fee. Publication of this play does not imply availability for performance. Both amateurs and professionals considering a production are strongly advised to apply to Samuel French before starting rehearsals, advertising, or booking a theatre. A licensing fee must be paid whether the title is presented for charity or gain and whether or not admission is charged. Professional/Stock licensing fees are quoted upon application to Samuel French.

No one shall make any changes in this title for the purpose of production. No part of this book may be reproduced, stored in a retrieval system, or transmitted in any form, by any means, now known or yet to be invented, including mechanical, electronic, photocopying, recording, videotaping, or otherwise, without the prior written permission of the publisher. No one shall upload this title, or part of this title, to any social media websites.

For all enquiries regarding motion picture, television, and other media rights, please contact Samuel French.

MUSIC USE NOTE

Licensees are solely responsible for obtaining formal written permission from copyright owners to use copyrighted music in the performance of this play and are strongly cautioned to do so. If no such permission is obtained by the licensee, then the licensee must use only original music that the licensee owns and controls. Licensees are solely responsible and liable for all music clearances and shall indemnify the copyright owners of the play(s) and their licensing agent, Samuel French, against any costs, expenses, losses and liabilities arising from the use of music by licensees. Please contact the appropriate music licensing authority in your territory for the rights to any incidental music.

IMPORTANT BILLING AND CREDIT REQUIREMENTS

If you have obtained performance rights to this title, please refer to your licensing agreement for important billing and credit requirements.

THE HOUSE OF FOG was first produced by Monkeys With Shotguns at the Etcetera Theatre, London in October 2009. The performance was directed by Peter Brammer and designed by Joseph Green, with lighting and sound by Peter Brammer and Dominic Ross. The cast was as follows:

NARRATOR	Johan Buckingham
TIMOTHY RACKONSFIELD	Matthew Groom
LUCY LACKENSPIEL/TRACEY SLAUGHTER	Claire Richardson
HAMPSHIRE	Robert Rowe
NANNY MARKSWORTH/FIONA HARRINGTON	Sarah Feathers
LADY RACKONSFIELD	Amy Ross
COUNT SILVIO/BILL SLAUGHTER	Tim Fordyce
GREGOR RACKINOV	Roberto Cavazos
CHARLOTTE RAVENSTILTH	Jessica Clark
GHOST	Roberto Cavazos

Voiceovers performed by members of the company.

This version of the play was first produced by Reppro at The Miller, London in April 2013. The performance was directed by Peter Brammer and Barney Hart Dyke, with lighting, design and sound by Barney Hart Dyke. The cast was as follows:

NARRATOR	Samuel Lewis
TIMOTHY RACKONSFIELD	James John Bryant
LUCY LACKENSPIEL/TRACEY SLAUGHTER	Jessica Gardner
HAMPSHIRE	David Clement-Horton
NANNY MARKSWORTH/FIONA HARRINGTON	Gina Sneesby
LADY RACKONSFIELD	Michelene Heine
COUNT SILVIO/BILL SLAUGHTER	Luca Pusceddu
GREGOR RACKINOV	Lee Ravitz/David Hempsted
CHARLOTTE RAVENSTILTH	Chania Belle

ACKNOWLEDGEMENT

Peter Brammer would like to thank Rachel Pidoux-Smith for her support and for creating the artwork for both productions of *The House of Fog*.

CHARACTERS

NARRATOR, elderly actor. Likes to voice his own opinion on the piece in front of the cast and audience. Firmly believes they are better than this.

TIMOTHY RACKONSFIELD, the unlikely romantic hero. Naïve, arrogant and a bit of a wimp.

LUCY LACKENSPIEL/TRACEY SLAUGHTER, con artist posing as Timothy's fiancée from Cheshire, but not all she seems.

HAMPSHIRE, the Rackonsfields' family butler. Slightly unnerving as to being covered in cobwebs and creeping up on people with a plate of macaroons.

NANNY MARKSWORTH/FIONA HARRINGTON, spy trailing Bill Slaughter posing undercover as the family nanny who disappeared. Having an affair with the gardener.

LADY RACKONSFIELD, Timothy's long suffering mother who has inherited Rackonsfield House and the fortune from her dead husband.

COUNT SILVIO/BILL SLAUGHTER, con artist posing as a friend of the Rackonsfields from Bavaria to murder the family and steal the fortune.

GREGOR RACKINOV, a gardener turned monster hunter trying to trail the beast that is ruining his hard work, unaware that it is in fact him. Having an affair with Fiona Harrington, super spy.

CHARLOTTE RAVENSTILTH, family friend and Timothy's childhood sweetheart.

GHOST, the ghost of Timothy's father, William Rackonsfield. Wants his death to be avenged but not optimistic about his son's efforts.

THE HOUSE OF FOG

Scene One

(A bare stage apart from an armchair downstage right with a large leather bound book on it. There is also a bush upstage right. Creepy music begins to play. As the stage starts to fill with smoke the music ends.)

VOICEOVER. You are sitting comfortably, yes? You are refreshed, at peace, comfortable, nothing can perturb you? Not here in a darkened theatre, smoke entering your nostrils. You are happy, content, there is nothing that can shatter your feeling of absolute security. Did you lock your doors? Latch your windows? Yes, you are safe, there is no room for superstition in your life…is there… *Is there?* You may want to cover your eyes as the horror of tonight's story unfolds. Nothing can prepare you for the terror as you enter the house of fog! Ha, ha, haaaaa.

*(Music plays, then there is a flash of lightning followed by a crash of thunder. The **NARRATOR** enters and staggers blindly through the fog grumbling, bumps into the chair, then picks up the large book and blows dust off the cover. He then opens it and blows dust off the pages. He breathes in and begins to cough uncontrollably. After a while he reads from the book.)*

NARRATOR. It was a foggy night.

(Pause)

Timothy Rackonsfield the third had decided that this night, October the thirty-first—

(Creepy music)

– he would take his fiancée Lucy Lackenspiel to his childhood home.

(**TIMOTHY** *and* **LUCY** *enter and make their way across the stage to where the* **NARRATOR** *is. They are both struggling to find their way through the imaginary fog.*)

TIMOTHY. Damned fog, I can't see a blasted thing.

LUCY. What fog?

TIMOTHY. This fog...

LUCY. Oh right, the fog. It is very thick.

TIMOTHY. It was never this thick before.

LUCY. You mean when you were an ickle baby boy.

TIMOTHY. I mean ever.

LUCY. Oh.

(*They reach the other end of the stage and exit behind the* **NARRATOR**.)

NARRATOR. As they reached the house the fog began to clear... (*He looks around at the vast amount of smoke still on the stage.*) ...slowly.

(*A light comes up on a large door.* **TIMOTHY** *and* **LUCY** *appear again. There is a long silence as they stare at the* **NARRATOR**.)

Well go on then...oh God, yes, sorry, my fault. They reach the door and knock heavily three times.

(**TIM** *knocks on the door three times. We hear three knocks.*)

LUCY. I'm uneasy.

NARRATOR. Lucy is uneasy.

(**TIM** *and* **LUCY** *both look at the* **NARRATOR**. *The* **NARRATOR** *exits.*)

LUCY. This place is creepy.

TIMOTHY. No creepier than your childhood home.

LUCY. My childhood home is not creepy.

TIMOTHY. It's a deserted farmhouse.

LUCY. So?

TIMOTHY. In Cheshire.

LUCY. And?

TIMOTHY. There are cows.

LUCY. It's a farm.

TIMOTHY. And hippos.

LUCY. A very special farm.

TIMOTHY. Never saw any though.

LUCY. What?

TIMOTHY. Cows or hippos.

LUCY. They go away for the winter.

TIMOTHY. Really? Fascinating.

> *(Pause.* **LUCY** *stares at* **TIMOTHY**. *After a while the door opens with a loud creak. A head pops round the door.)*

HAMPSHIRE. Good evening, can I help you?

TIMOTHY. Hello, Hampshire. It's me, Master Timothy.

HAMPSHIRE. That is impossible, sir. Master Timothy is… dead.

> *(Burst of creepy music)*

TIMOTHY. But I am Timothy.

> *(Long pause.* **HAMPSHIRE** *opens the door wider.)*

HAMPSHIRE. Impossible, he died last year, sir, he drowned in the lake..

> *(Music)*

TIMOTHY. But it's me…what lake? What's going on?

HAMPSHIRE. I am joking, sir.

> *(***LUCY** *and* **TIMOTHY** *enter beyond the door.* **HAMPSHIRE** *pushes the door offstage. Inside there are a couple of chairs by a fireplace.)*

TIMOTHY. Oh, Hampshire you old rascal. Lucy, meet Hampshire, our butler and faithful friend. Hampshire, meet Lucy, my fiancée.

HAMPSHIRE. Pleased to meet you, Madam.

LUCY. Oh please call me Lucy.

HAMPSHIRE. Very well... Lucy.

TIMOTHY. So Hampshire, where's Haplespeer?

HAMPSHIRE. Haplespeer is dead, sir.

TIMOTHY. Pulling my leg again, eh?

HAMPSHIRE. No sir.

(Burst of creepy music)

TIMOTHY. Haplespeer, dead?

HAMPSHIRE. Yes sir, dead.

(Music)

TIMOTHY. Dead?

HAMPSHIRE. Dead sir, yes.

(Music)

TIMOTHY. You're not joking

HAMPSHIRE. No sir.

(Music)

TIMOTHY. Dead.

(Long pause)

HAMPSHIRE. If you would both like to warm yourself by the fire, while I prepare your room.

(TIMOTHY *and* **LUCY** *sit by the fire.* **HAMPSHIRE** *exits.)*

TIMOTHY. I can't believe it.

LUCY. What?

TIMOTHY. Haplespeer dead.

(Music. Pause. They look towards the lighting box and shake their heads.)

LUCY. Was he a close friend?

TIMOTHY. Yes he used to give me piggyback rides, play tennis with me and give me sweets, tell me dark stories of the north, wipe my bu...nose, bandage my knees when I had a boo boo... No wait a minute...that was

Hampshire. Haplespeer always used to freak me out, staring at me the whole time.

LUCY. I can't believe you grew up here. It's so big.

TIMOTHY. It's huge isn't it?

*(The **NARRATOR** enters.)*

NARRATOR. Lucy and Timothy looked around the vast and yes…foggy house. After a while an old woman entered and as she hobbled toward the couple Timothy leapt out of his chair and ran towards her.

*(**TIMOTHY** has leapt out of his chair and is hugging the old woman. She is motionless.)*

TIMOTHY. Nanny Marksworth!

MARKSWORTH. Master Timothy, you've come home.

TIMOTHY. Yes I have, aren't you pleased?

MARKSWORTH. Why?

TIMOTHY. What?

MARKSWORTH. Why have you come home?

TIMOTHY. I wanted my fiancée to meet Ma and Pa. Which reminds me…

NARRATOR. Timothy introduces Nanny Marksworth to Lucy.

TIMOTHY. I can do it myself you know!

NARRATOR. You're sure?

TIMOTHY. Yes!

NARRATOR. Okay, fine. I'm going. You do realise I'm the glue? I hold this drivel together. Without me the audience wouldn't know what was going on, assuming they can see through the fog!

TIMOTHY. Are you finished?

NARRATOR. …Yes! Yes I am.

*(**NARRATOR** exits.)*

TIMOTHY. Nanny Marksworth, this is my fiancée Lucy.

MARKSWORTH. Fer.

TIMOTHY. No Lucy.

MARKSWORTH. Fer.

TIMOTHY. No, Lucy Lackenspiel, not Lucifer.

MARKSWORTH. Lucifer! Where?

TIMOTHY. Nowhere.

(MARKSWORTH points at LUCY.)

MARKSWORTH. There!

(She runs off, mumbling loudly to herself.)

LUCY. Are all your family this friendly?

TIMOTHY. She's not family…she was my nanny.

(HAMPSHIRE enters.)

TIMOTHY. Hampshire, you old devil.

HAMPSHIRE. …Yes sir, quite. Your mother awaits you in the drawing room.

TIMOTHY. What about Pa?

HAMPSHIRE. Your father is unavailable at this moment, sir.

TIMOTHY. Really? Oh well I guess I'd better say hello to Ma. Lead the way, Hampshire, you old rascal!

(He slaps HAMPSHIRE on the arm.)

HAMPSHIRE. Mmm. If you would like to follow me?

(He leads them out.)

(Blackout)

Scene Two

(Creepy music plays. **NARRATOR** *enters and spotlight comes up. He moves into it. During the following speech* **LADY RACKONSFIELD** *enters and, finding no chair, steals the* **NARRATOR***'s.)*

NARRATOR. Hampshire led Lucy and Timothy down the vast, labyrinth-like, and... *(he sighs)* foggy corridors. Portraits lined the walls. Lucy would shudder as she passed the pictures – she was sure they were watching her. Yes, watching her, the oldest cliché there is, I know, this thing was written in the early nineteen hundreds you know. Finally Hampshire stopped and opened the door to the drawing room.

*(***NARRATOR*** goes to sit down and falls over. Lights come up on the drawing room and a seated* **LADY MABEL RACKONSFIELD***.)*

HAMPSHIRE. Master Timothy and his fiancée, Your Ladyship.

MABEL. Thank you, Hampshire.

TIMOTHY. Yes, you little...

HAMPSHIRE. Rascal, sir?

TIMOTHY. Yes.

HAMPSHIRE. Thank you, sir.

MABEL. That will be all, Hampshire.

HAMPSHIRE. Very good, Your Ladyship.

*(***MABEL*** gets up and runs towards* **TIMOTHY***. She embraces him, almost knocking him over.)*

MABEL. My baby's come home!

TIMOTHY. Mother. Err, Mother? Mother, this is lovely and all but I can't breathe.

*(***TIMOTHY*** collapses.)*

MABEL. Oh sorry.

TIMOTHY. Mother, I would like to introduce my fiancée Lucy Lackenspiel. Lucy, my mother, Lady Mabel Racksonfield.

(**LUCY** *curtseys.*)

LUCY. Pleased to meet you, Your Ladyship. Timothy has told me so much about you all.

MABEL. He has?

LUCY. Yes, all good, I can assure you.

MABEL. I am pleased to hear it. Lackenspiel is an intriguing name. What is it, Swedish?

LUCY. No, it's an old Cheshire name, as Cheshire as cheese.

(Pause)

TIMOTHY. So how's everything?

MABEL. You have chosen to visit in dark, troubled times, Timothy, dark, troubled times.

(**NARRATOR** *enters.*)

NARRATOR. Mabel explained that Timothy had returned in dark, troubled times.

TIMOTHY. Yes she's done that bit; get on with the next bit.

NARRATOR. Look, I'm getting sick of this. I am the narrator. I have a direct link with the audience. I establish and clarify finer points of the story, so let me do my job. Okay?

(Everyone on stage nods.)

Good, I'm pleased that's settled. Oh, and that, missy, is my chair!

(Long pause. They all stare at him.)

Oh no, I'm done...carry on.

TIMOTHY. What on earth do you mean, Mother?

MABEL. This house is cursed, haunted by evil spirits. The house was built on a gypsy settlement, unfortunately literally on top of the gypsies as they slept, and though flattened they managed to curse the house and much earlier the site was the place of a great battle so it was already pretty haunted anyway. Also... Timothy, your father William is dead.

TIMOTHY. What? No!

(LUCY holds him. They continue the scene as the NARRATOR speaks.)

NARRATOR. Mabel explained that William, independent as he was, had died while making tea in the afternoon, a random flying teabag...

(He shrugs.)

...hit his eye, blinding him. As he stumbled aimlessly around he slipped on that same teabag and fell down the concrete stairs leading to the cold damp concrete cellar floor. This fall killed him instantly...oh no, he survived, but then his collection of European ceremonial swords shaped like vegetables fell on him. He was killed by a lethal piece of asparagus that hit him on the head and a leek plunged deep into his heart.

(Pause)

(Looking into the wings)... A leek? A leek? What kind of idiot picked up his crayon and scrawled this tripe? And more importantly why didn't somebody stop him? I played Lear, you know?

TIMOTHY. Yeah in a tour of residental homes!

NARRATOR. What? Yes, maybe so, but still Lear, Lear!

(He exits. TIMOTHY, with his arm over his eyes, speaks)

TIMOTHY. Pa killed by a vagrant...

(He sneaks a peek at the audience then replaces his arm.)

...teabag.

MABEL. Now his spirit roams this house, you can hear him sipping tea made with the bag that killed him.

(Pause)

LUCY. Did they have teabags in the early nineteen hundreds?

(They all look at her.)

Sorry.

MABEL. Oh how I miss him.

(A mysterious figure emerges from behind a curtain, **COUNT SILVIO**.*)*

SILVIO. We all do. Come...

*(***MABEL** *embraces him. He places his hands on her bottom.)*

TIMOTHY. Who are you?

SILVIO. Forgive me for not introducing myself. I am Count Silvio, a friend of your father's.

(He holds out his hand. **TIMOTHY** *ignores it.)*

TIMOTHY. He never mentioned you.

SILVIO. We were at school together but reunited during your absence. He contacted me when the curse became severe.

MABEL. Silvio is an exorcist and paranormal expert.

TIMOTHY. Really?

SILVIO. Yes.

TIMOTHY. Is that so?

SILVIO. Yes.

TIMOTHY. Really?

SILVIO. Yes.

TIMOTHY. Is that so?

SILVIO. Yes.

TIMOTHY. Really?

MABEL. Stop that, Timothy!

TIMOTHY. Yes, Mother.

*(***SILVIO** *moves towards* **LUCY**.*)*

SILVIO. My dear, I don't believe we've been introduced?

(He kisses her hand.)

LUCY. My name is...

*(***TIMOTHY**, *interrupting, puts his arm around* **LUCY**.*)*

TIMOTHY. Her name is Lucy, Lucy Lackenspiel, and she happens to be my fiancée!

SILVIO. I offer my congratulations to you both. Lackenspiel, a marvellous name. Is it Swedish?

TIMOTHY. No it's Chesish…

(They all look at him.)

TIMOTHY. What?

LUCY. It's an old Cheshire name, Count.

SILVIO. Is that an old Cheshire accent, too?

*(**LUCY** looks embarrassed.)*

You are a lucky man, Timothy… Timothy sounds so formal, may I call you Tim?

TIMOTHY. No!

MABEL. Don't be so rude, Tim.

TIMOTHY. But Mother…

MABEL. Silvio is here to help us.

TIMOTHY. But…

MABEL. Hush!

*(**NANNY MARKSWORTH** rushes in.)*

MARKSWORTH. Dinner is served!

*(She spies **LUCY** and runs off screaming.)*

MABEL. What's gotten into Nanny?

TIMOTHY. She thinks Lucy is the devil.

MABEL. I see. Shall we?

(They all exit.)

(Blackout)

Scene Three

(Creepy music plays. Lights come up on **GREGOR RACKINOV**. **NARRATOR** *takes back his chair and sits, satisfied. Then he remembers, jumps up and moves the bush centre stage.)*

NARRATOR. Meanwhile, in the gardens of Rackonsfield house, the gardener Gregor Rackinov makes plans for the night ahead.

GREGOR. Right, tonight I stay here in the gardens; tonight I will be ready for the vile beast that has been destroying my hard work. Trampling my flower beds, tearing up my geraniums and the worst of all…

(He steps in something.)

…defecating on my shrubbery. I have my pitchfork, my shovel, the shears and a…bucket. I will be here all night if need be. I sense evil in this garden and I quash evil at every turn. I hear someone or something…

(He jumps into a bush. **NANNY MARKSWORTH** *enters carrying a tray.)*

MARKSWORTH. Gregor? Supper's ready, Gregor? Gregor?

*(***GREGOR*** emerges from the bush. He grabs her, she spins round and they kiss.)*

GREGOR. I have been waiting for that all day.

MARKSWORTH. Oooh you are bad, kiss me again!

(He does.)

Again.

(He does.)

Ooooh.

(She pushes him into the bush and jumps in after him. Then, making sexy sounds, they exit upstage with the bush. The bush doesn't fit.)

GREGOR. Other way.

(They exit downstage.)

NARRATOR. Nanny Marksworth and Gregor were attracted to one another. Well, d'uh!

(Blackout)

Scene Four

(Lights come up on **NARRATOR** *who hasn't moved. He is scratching himself when he notices the lights are up.)*

NARRATOR. After sitting down to dinner...

*(***TIMOTHY, LUCY, LADY RACKONSFIELD, COUNT SILVIO** *and* **HAMPSHIRE** *enter. They all sit except for* **HAMPSHIRE** *who stands.)*

Lucy comments on how young Lady Rackonsfield looks...

*(***NARRATOR** *flashes a look at the audience.)*

MABEL. In my day women became mothers at a very early age. In my case I was eight.

*(***NARRATOR** *throws his hands up in despair.)*

NARRATOR. After eating, and just before dessert, Lady Rackonsfield reveals that she and Count Silvio are married.

TIMOTHY. Egads! What were you thinking, Mother? You hardly know this man!

HAMPSHIRE. Macaroon, sir?

TIMOTHY. Jesus! Oh it's you, Hampshire... Sorry, what did you say?

HAMPSHIRE. Would you like a macaroon?

TIMOTHY. Oh... I— yes, thank you, Hampshire. Mother?

MABEL. I can't live in this house on my own, Timothy, not with all the unsettled spirits and your father stalking the halls with his...teacup. The count was there for me when I needed him.

TIMOTHY. Yes your timing, Count, is impeccable.

LUCY. Timothy, be nice.

TIMOTHY. Don't tell me you are on his side.

*(***COUNT SILVIO** *winks at* **LUCY.** *She giggles.)*

Lucy, are you mad? This man waltzes into my childhood home claiming to be my father's friend, marries my mother and now you are sharing little moments with him.

SILVIO. Your father told me you were the suspicious type.

TIMOTHY. Your situation and actions aren't helping my suspicions, Count. With all due respect, sir, I do not trust you.

SILVIO. With all due respect, Master Timothy, your distrust is of no concern to me.

HAMPSHIRE. Miss Charlotte Ravenstilth.

NARRATOR. Ravenstilth? Didn't anyone in the nineteen hundreds have a normal name – Smith, Barker – what is it with these names Rackonsfield, Lackenspiel, I ask you?

(He looks at the cast who are all staring at him. He exits.)

TIMOTHY. Lottie! What is she doing here?

MABEL. I invited her.

TIMOTHY. What, why?

LUCY. Who is she?

TIMOTHY. She's my…my…

MABEL. She is Timothy's childhood sweetheart.

TIMOTHY. Mother.

LUCY. Oh. I see.

TIMOTHY. It was a long time ago, it means nothing now.

LUCY. Why are you so upset that she is here then?

SILVIO. Yes, why are you so aggravated – do tell us?

TIMOTHY. Don't you start…you, you bearded…brute…

*(**HAMPSHIRE** brings in **LOTTIE** and a chair for her to sit on.)*

LOTTIE. Thank you, Hampshire.

HAMPSHIRE. Miss.

LOTTIE. Hello, Timothy.

TIMOTHY. Lottie.

LOTTIE. Thank you for inviting me, Lady Rackonsfield, I haven't been here since the wedding.

TIMOTHY. Hmmph.

MABEL. Timothy! Don't you have anything to say to Lottie?

(He moves forward. The cast freezes.)

TIMOTHY. So much to say: why I left, why I never wrote, how I still love her. But no, I'm with Lucy now. Oh, Lottie.

(He moves back. The cast unfreezes.)

TIMOTHY. Lottie?

LOTTIE. Yes, Timothy?

TIMOTHY. Why are you here?

MABEL. Timothy!

LOTTIE. Well, your mother invited me and having not seen you for so long I thought I'd say hello…

(Long pause)

LOTTIE. Hello.

TIMOTHY. Well, since you're here, Lottie, I would like you to meet my fiancée, Lucy Lackenspiel…

LOTTIE. Fiancée?

TIMOTHY. Yes, we are to be married.

LOTTIE. Married… I… I

*(**LOTTIE** comes forward. The cast freezes.)*

A long time ago, when the summers were warm and golden, our hearts were pure and entwined. You see, we loved one another. Timbo and I were inseparable. I still remember that day in the field where we shared our first kiss. That was the most exhilarating and arousing experience of my life. Then he left. He wrote and I replied, then nothing. I decided to move on. I met Billy, then Gregory, Harry, Bert, Nigel, Martin, Terry, Kenneth…oh, and Barry. Then I realized all they were good for was a bit of fun… lots of fun…

(She giggles.)

…What I had with Timbo, though, was different, pure, real and fluffy. After the pitchfork incident – Barry liked to try new things – my parents left the farm, you see the pigs were no longer profitable after word got around that Barry had…interfered. When I found out, I asked Barry to leave…which he did…with a few piglets, possibly his own, we weren't sure. The Rackonsfields took me in. I stayed in Timbo's bed…

(She giggles.)

…and remembered. There I vowed to keep myself for him, no more farm boys who only wanted to make bacon, literally in Barry's case. I dreamed he would come back for me and we'd be married and fluffy, have fifteen children and live happily ever after. Now he is back, but with this Lucy…

(She goes back. The cast unfreezes.)

Lackenspiel, is that Swedish?

TIMOTHY AND LUCY. No.

LUCY. I am from Cheshire.

LOTTIE. Really?

(LOTTIE looks at LADY RACKONSFIELD, LADY RACKONSFIELD shakes her head.)

MABEL. I trust you will be staying the whole weekend?

LOTTIE. If it's not too much trouble.

MABEL. Not at all.

TIMOTHY. Not much.

MABEL. Timothy!

TIMOTHY. What?

MABEL. I have had enough of this attitude, young man. If we didn't have guests I would spank you so hard your eyes would water. You are not too old for a good hiding. If you continue to be downright rude to our guests I will have no choice but to send you to your room until you have decided to be civil. Things haven't been easy for me recently and the count and Charlotte have been there for me. The count is a kind, caring and daring lover...

(They all immediately look up.)

...Charlotte was there the day your father passed away and made me a cup of tea which was a little upsetting considering the circumstances of your father's death, but she wasn't to know. Now I suggest you buck up your ideas, Timmykins, or I will not be tucking you in tonight!

(TIMOTHY *is silent for a moment...his bottom lip wobbles and he runs off.)*

SILVIO. Well said.

MABEL. Maybe I was a bit harsh, but he was being so rude.

LUCY. I...er...I?

MABEL. Oh, go after him dear!

*(***LUCY** *exits.)*

Sorry you had to see that, Lottie, but it was the only thing to do.

LOTTIE. Timmykins?

MABEL. Our pet name for him. His father came up with it when he was a baby, he came up with it while making... tea.

(She cries. **SILVIO** *holds her.)*

SILVIO. Shall we retire for the evening?

MABEL. Oh yes.

(They leave canoodling, **LADY RACKONSFIELD** *is giggling.)*

MABEL. *(offstage)* Oooh Count!

LOTTIE. Hampshire?

HAMPSHIRE. Miss?

LOTTIE. Is my room prepared?

HAMPSHIRE. Yes, miss, in the West Wing.
LOTTIE. Good.
   (Blackout.)

Scene Five

*(**TIMOTHY** and **LUCY** are sitting on the bed. **TIMOTHY**'s head is in her lap. He is sobbing and **LUCY** is comforting him. **NARRATOR** enters.)*

NARRATOR. Upstairs, Lucy comforts an upset... Timmykins. Sorry, couldn't resist.

(He exits.)

LUCY. It's all right, my darling. You are upset, it's understandable in the circumstances. I think your mother was very unfair.

TIMOTHY. She was so mean...

LUCY. I know.

TIMOTHY. In front of all those people...

LUCY. I know.

TIMOTHY. I've just lost my father...

LUCY. Sssh, its okay.

TIMOTHY. And my stepfather's Bavarian!

*(He cries uncontrollably. **LUCY** lifts his head up.)*

LUCY. You still have me, and I will love you forever... *(She kisses him.)*

TIMOTHY. Will you?

LUCY. Yes. *(She nuzzles his neck.)*

TIMOTHY. And you won't call me Timmykins?

LUCY. Only if you ask me to?

TIMOTHY. Oh, Lucy.

(They kiss and cuddle. Suddenly there is a loud moan.)

LUCY. What was that?

TIMOTHY. What, what?

*(**LUCY** looks confused.)*

TIMOTHY. I mean what was what?

LUCY. That moan.

TIMOTHY. I thought it was you.

LUCY. No.

TIMOTHY. It was probably nothing.

(They continue kissing. Again there is a moan.)

LUCY. See? Please go see what it is.

TIMOTHY. But…we're going to… Oh, okay…

NARRATOR. Timothy went into the hallway and sure enough nothing was there. He was about to return to his room when there was another loud moan. I said, another loud moan…

(There is a loud moan.)

TIMOTHY. Hello?

NARRATOR. There was no reply.

TIMOTHY. I say, is anyone there?

NARRATOR. No reply.

TIMOTHY. They can tell, you know.

NARRATOR. Don't… start with me.

TIMOTHY. Sorry.

NARRATOR. He went to re-enter the bedroom when suddenly the candles blew out…

(Blackout)

Oh for God's— *(loudly)* the moon shone brightly through the windows.

(Lights come up)

Suddenly the windows blew open and started clattering loudly as a mighty wind swept though the hallway. Timothy ran for the door…

TIMOTHY. Lucy, unlock the door!

NARRATOR. She didn't… As Timothy stood frozen with fear, a terrible moaning could be heard from the other end of the hallway. The wind grew stronger and the clattering of the windows became a deafening roar. Timothy's eyes widened as blood-curdling shivers went up and down his spine. Gripped with terror, he stared down the empty hallway, all the while demons toying with his fragile, unsettled soul. Then he heard it. A sound that chilled him to the very core of his being, a sound more terrifying than any that had gone before it, scarier than any moan or scream...what he heard was truly monstrous...the gentle tinkle of a teaspoon against a china cup. His father had arrived. Then without warning his terrifying, ungodly, unspeakably horrific spectre appeared...

(An actor enters covered in a sheet with eyeholes.)

Oh come on! That's it? That's the shock? Victorian answer to Shakespeare, they said, relaunch your career, they said. Please. Enough, I'm going.

(He exits.)

GHOST. Timothy.

TIMOTHY. Father?

GHOST. Timothy, my son.

TIMOTHY. Father, is it you?

GHOST. Of course it's me, you simpleton, who'd you think it was, the ghost of Christmas past...?

TIMOTHY. Well...

GHOST. Shut up, you lily-livered, perfume-wearing pansy, I have something to tell you. Though don't know what good it'll do you're about as helpful as a toenail.

*(**TIMOTHY**'s lip starts to wobble.)*

GHOST. Don't cry, you wimp.

TIMOTHY. Why are you being so mean to me, Pa?

GHOST. Don't 'Pa' me, you toffee-nosed twit, I swear you were adopted. Anyway, I'm dead, I've got a right to be mean, because you see, snot-boy... I was murdered.

(Creepy music)

TIMOTHY. Murdered?

(Creepy music)

GHOST. Yes.

TIMOTHY. Murdered?

(Creepy music)

GHOST. Yes, look, we've established that, murdered…by Count Silvio.

TIMOTHY. I knew it!

GHOST. No you didn't.

TIMOTHY. What?

GHOST. Know, they knew, we knew, you didn't – you are just a lacklustre, confused little spoilt brat… Will you stop gaping at me like a comatose goldfish?

TIMOTHY. Sorry, I've never seen a ghost. Let alone my father's.

GHOST. Stop calling me your father, one of the lady ghosts might overhear and even though they're dead they like a man to have no ties.

TIMOTHY. But you're not wearing a t—

GHOST. Shut up. You'd think some of my intelligence would have rubbed off… You're gawping again.

TIMOTHY. Sorry it's just…you're a ghost!

GHOST. Course I am, why do you think my voice is coming over the speakers? There are loads of ghosts in this house, cheesed-off gypsies mainly. Avenge my death… oh, do what you like, you'll probably make a mess of it anyway.

(He starts to exit.)

TIMOTHY. Don't worry, Pa, I'll avenge your murder!

*(**GHOST** turns to him, pauses and walks off. **SILVIO** enters.)*

SILVIO. Murder?

TIMOTHY. Yes, murder, does that word make you nervous… Count?

SILVIO. One, two, oh sorry, you were addressing me. Why would a silly little word like murder upset me?

TIMOTHY. You'll find out soon enough. I am going for a walk.

SILVIO. At this hour?

TIMOTHY. Yes.
SILVIO. Really?
TIMOTHY. Yes.
SILVIO. Right now?
TIMOTHY. Yes.
SILVIO. Very well.

(NARRATOR enters.)

NARRATOR. Yes, I'm back… What can I say, it's cold out there! Timothy strode off down the corridor, revenge firmly set in his mind. As he left, Silvio knocked on the bedroom door, which opened. He crept inside. Meanwhile, in the garden…

(NANNY MARKSWORTH and GREGOR are lying against the bushes. Their clothes and hair are ruffled. Beside NANNY MARKSWORTH is her wig. She is now FIONA HARRINGTON, super-spy.)

GREGOR. Why do you pretend to be an old, mad woman? You are so, how you say, fox-like?

FIONA. I need to hide my identity, otherwise my cover would be blown and I'd never catch evil Bill Slaughter, a.k.a. Count Silvio.

GREGOR. How come you haven't caught him yet?

FIONA. I'm waiting for him to slip up, then I'll be all over him.

GREGOR. As opposed to all over me. What happened to the real—?

FIONA. Nanny Marksworth? Well, I turned up to turn her over to my superiors and she ran off, did us a favour really. Someone's coming, quick.

(They dive into the bushes. TIMOTHY and HAMPSHIRE enter.)

TIMOTHY. I appreciate your company, old man.

HAMPSHIRE. Sir.

TIMOTHY. You see my father came to me as a ghost just now and told me Count Silvio murdered him and I'm to avenge his death and I was just wondering what your thoughts were?

HAMPSHIRE. Excuse me, sir, I believe I hear a cuckoo.

(HAMPSHIRE exits.)

TIMOTHY. Hampshire...well, where are you going?

(We hear a terrible roar.)

FIONA. Here we go again, you animal.

(She jumps out of the bushes dressed as Nanny Marksworth and runs off. Then GREGOR rises out of the bushes as the MONSTER and goes to grab TIMOTHY. NARRATOR runs on.)

NARRATOR. Whoah, whoah, whoah, stop, you're getting ahead of yourselves.

(They freeze.)

Gregor had once again become the feral beast you see before you. What? Use your imaginations, people! Nanny Marksworth, knowing his secret, got away early. Timothy was not so lucky.

(GREGOR *bites* **TIMOTHY**'s *hand.* **TIMOTHY** *runs off crying. Blackout)*

Scene Six

(LUCY and SILVIO are sitting on the bed. SILVIO is using his real accent, the accent of BILL SLAUGHTER. LUCY is also using her real accent, the accent of TRACEY SLAUGHTER, BILL's daughter.)

TRACEY. Where's Timothy?

BILL. He went out muttering something about murder…

TRACEY. Murder! You think he knows?

BILL. Well it doesn't matter, he'll be dead soon, there's a wild beast prowling around out there.

TRACEY. I don't like this place. I heard moaning. Timothy went to see what it was.

BILL. That was his mother…

TRACEY. Really? Eww!

BILL. I know…

TRACEY. Timothy's more a breather…

BILL. Not entirely sure I needed to know that.

TRACEY. Sorry.

(During the next few moments. NANNY MARKSWORTH as FIONA HARRINGTON in a balaclava enters at the back of the stage, creeping as if on a window ledge.)

BILL. Soon, however, they will all be dead and the Rackonsfield fortune will be ours. First I kill the father, then the son and then I'll kill that lush of a mother of his.

(FIONA makes a gesture as if to say yes and wobbles, but manages to resteady herself.)

TRACEY. The sooner the better, I'm sick of this accent.

BILL. You chose it.

TRACEY. Why should you be the only one to be European? I wanted a touch of class for a change.

BILL. Swedish, fine, but insisting you come from Cheshire?... Nothing more suspicious than a Swedish girl in Cheshire.

TRACEY. Oh, and Count Silvio is perfectly believable.

BILL. With these kind of people, yes.

(A sobbing is heard.)

BILL. What's that?

TRACEY. Sounds like Tim.

BILL. Right, we have a job to do.

(They exit. **FIONA** *hurriedly exits via the windowsill.)*

Scene Seven

(The garden. **GREGOR** *is crouched in a squatting position. He is battling with his inner* **MONSTER**. *He switches from one to the other during the scene.)*

GREGOR. My flowers, ruined again. Why can I never catch him, what is this thing?

MONSTER. I am the thing.

GREGOR. Who are you?

MONSTER. I am you.

GREGOR. Who?

MONSTER. You?

GREGOR. Me?

MONSTER. Yes.

GREGOR. But how?

MONSTER. Remember that nasty wolf that bit you a few years ago?

GREGOR. Oooh yes, big black thing, nasty, lovely fur but vicious.

MONSTER. That was me, I used my bite to enter your body. I could go into detail but I won't, it's tricky, all to do with myths and stuff.

GREGOR. But why didn't I know?

MONSTER. You weren't supposed to. Anyway, I'm off now. You're getting a bit old and a bit hairy, so when we bit someone younger and not so hairy I latched on, but I thought I'd say hi in my final moments and thanks for having me.

GREGOR. But you destroyed my garden and now you leave. What happens to me?

MONSTER. Oh well, now you'll die once I've gone, my life force gave you an extra few years. You know that heart attack you had?

GREGOR. Yes.

MONSTER. It killed you...

GREGOR. But you can't leave. I have a lover, I don't want to die, I have too much... well, a bit to live for.

MONSTER. She'd leave you. You see, the curse takes over when you – you know.

GREGOR. I won't let you leave.

MONSTER. It's ironic, isn't it? You wanted me dead, but now you know I'm you, you want me to stay.

(**GREGOR** *starts thrashing around.*)

GREGOR. No, you must stay...

MONSTER. I'm off...

GREGOR. No.

MONSTER. Yes!

GREGOR. Stay here!

MONSTER. Stop it, you're making a scene!

GREGOR. I won't, I won't let you leave me to die!

MONSTER. You've had a good innings, accept it.

GREGOR. No!

MONSTER. You're behaving like a child!

GREGOR. I don't want to die, it's not fair, you stay, keep me alive.

MONSTER. Look, you're not going to win, in fact all this thrashing around doesn't do anything, just makes you look a bit silly.

GREGOR. So there's nothing I can do?

MONSTER. Nope.

GREGOR. Not even this?

(**GREGOR** *thrashes about again.*)

MONSTER. You're wasting your time.

GREGOR. I don't care. You are not going to leave...

MONSTER. See ya!

GREGOR. No, wait...

(**GREGOR** *drops down, dead.*)

Scene Eight

(The entrance hall. **TIMOTHY** *is sitting caressing his bitten hand. The* **NARRATOR** *enters.)*

NARRATOR. In the house Timothy sobbed loudly as he clutched his bleeding hand. Timothy's tears told of his ordeal on a night he'd never forget...and the career he'd never have...

TIMOTHY. What?

NARRATOR. Face it, we're finished the minute the reviews come out...bang, the dream is over.

TIMOTHY. Are you quite finished?

NARRATOR. Yes, we all are.

*(***HAMPSHIRE** *enters with a plate.)*

HAMPSHIRE. Macaroon, sir?

TIMOTHY. What? No! Can't you see I'm bleeding to death? Some god-awful thing bit me in the grounds...after you left. Some friend you are, Hampshire, leaving me to the mercy of wild beasts. Here I am bleeding to—

*(***HAMPSHIRE** *begins to leave.)*

What? Well where are you going now? Hampshire, get back here... Hampshire...!

*(***HAMPSHIRE** *exits.* **BILL** *and* **TRACEY** *enter.)*

BILL. Right, there he is...you distract him and I'll creep up behind him and throttle him.

TRACEY. Okay, but be quick, I'm sick of this accent, and him.

*(***BILL** *tiptoes out of* **TIMOTHY***'s view.)*

TIMOTHY. Lucy!

LUCY. Timothy.

(She goes towards him and hugs him.)

LUCY. What happened to your hand? You're bleeding.

TIMOTHY. Something in the grounds attacked me. It was horrible, huge, smelly and hairy...it—

(**BILL** *throttles* **TIMOTHY**.)

NARRATOR. At that moment, Bill Slaughter wrapped his hands around Timothy's throat. Timothy struggled and managed to let out a scream. Lady Rackonsfield, Lottie, Hampshire and then a terrifying spectre...

(*Actor in a sheet enters.*)

...appeared

GHOST. Oh I knew he'd mess it up, idiot!

(*He exits.*)

MABEL. Count Silvio, put my son down this instant!

(**BILL** *drops* **TIMOTHY**.)

BILL. (*as* **SILVIO**) I'm sorry, he was trying to kill Lucy and I leapt to her defence.

TRACEY. (*as* **LUCY**) It's true!

TIMOTHY. It damn bloody well is not...

MABEL. Timothy, how could you?

TIMOTHY. I didn't.

LOTTIE. I believe him.

MABEL. Count?

BILL. He was blind with rage...he—

NARRATOR. Then at that point, making a dramatic entrance, Fiona arrived.

(**FIONA** *jumps in from offstage dressed as* **NANNY MARKSWORTH**.)

Oh please, that's dramatic? Couldn't we have had a pyrotechnic or something?

FIONA. Quiet. That's enough, Count Silvio, or should I say Bill Slaughter?

ALL. Nanny Marksworth!

(**FIONA** *takes off her wig.*)

FIONA. The name's Harrington... Fiona Harrington, super spy.

NARRATOR. Oh Jesus!

(He exits. **FIONA** *jumps about and grabs* **BILL** *and* **LUCY**.*)*

FIONA. Lady Rackonsfield, you were taken in by a skilled conman and his daughter. First he killed your husband, Timothy was next on the list then you, Your Ladyship. He wanted the fortune, the house, everything.

TIMOTHY. Lucy?

TRACEY. My name's Tracey.

TIMOTHY. Your accent?

TRACEY. This is my real accent, you twit. What on earth made you think someone like me would want to marry a stuck up, moronic crybaby like you?

TIMOTHY. But—

FIONA. Come on, you two.

(She drags them off.)

BILL. I'll be back!

LOTTIE. Whatever happened to the real Nanny Marksworth?

(A scream is heard offstage.)

HAMPSHIRE. I believe she may be back, miss. Macaroon?

LOTTIE. No thank you. Will you go check on Nanny Marksworth?

HAMPSHIRE. Miss, I shall.

(He exits.)

HAMPSHIRE. *(offstage)* Nanny Marksworth... Macaroon?

MABEL. I feel such a fool.

LOTTIE. You weren't to know. Timothy, you were right.

(She walks over to him. His bottom lip is wobbling.)

Oh, you're bleeding. Timothy, what's the matter?

TIMOTHY. Lucy, she wasn't Lucy at all she...she...

LOTTIE. I know...

TIMOTHY. Lottie, I've been a fool...
LOTTIE. You always have been.
TIMOTHY. I'm sorry. You know I've always loved you.
LOTTIE. I love you too.
MABEL. I knew it. After all, you two were made for each other.

(They look at her.)

Not literally of course.

TIMOTHY. Is there room in your heart for a damn fool?
LOTTIE. Always has been.

(They embrace and kiss. It gets passionate.)

MABEL. Oh my...
NARRATOR. So everything worked out for the best, albeit neatly. What did you expect? A clever twist?
MABEL. What do you mean everything worked out? There are still ghosts stalking the halls!
NARRATOR. Well yes, but the wild beast is no more, and justice has been served. Anyway, if the ghosts are just people in sheets there's nothing to worry about...
MABEL. I've had enough of your sarcasm. Some of us have actually worked hard tonight, not just stood there and made snide comments.
NARRATOR. Don't you have a go at me... I played Lear and had a brilliant career before this wreck.
MABEL. Brilliant career, what off, off, off Broadway and the fringe of the fringe? Oooh, big whoop!
NARRATOR. I'll big whoop you in a minute. Look here, Missy...

*(They exit arguing. **TIMOTHY** and **LOTTIE** are still kissing. Blackout. **TIMOTHY** howls.)*

LOTTIE. Oh my... Timothy!
HAMPSHIRE. Macaroon?

End of play

www.ingramcontent.com/pod-product-compliance
Lightning Source LLC
Chambersburg PA
CBHW070453050426
42450CB00012B/3264